AROUND MISSION

photographs by

GRAHAM DOWDEN

Gyre & Gimble Publishers
33644 Cherry Ave
Mission, British Columbia V2V 2V6
http://grahamdowden.ca

Cataloguing in Publication Data © 2007

Dowden, Graham, 1940–

      Around Mission / photographs by Graham Dowden
      (includes text; 128 pp.)

1. Mission (B.C.)—Pictorial works. 2. Photography, artistic. 3. Photography—British Columbia.   I. Title.

FC3812 D69 2007   AACR2
971.1/04/0222 22

ISBN 978-0-9782328-0-1

Designed by Graham Dowden

Printed in Canada by Friesens 2007

Twas brillig and the slithy toves ...

FOR JUDY

INTRODUCTION

This book came out of a conversation. I was standing in an art gallery, happy enough that some of my pictures were on its walls, but telling a fellow that it was all very nice to be getting a show now and then, yet what one really wanted to do was bring out a *book*. I mentioned how daunting it was, when one had arrived at a certain age still without any reputation of note, to face the prospect of convincing a legitimate publisher to take on one's very first body of work.

"Pshaw!" he said. "Publish it yourself!"

"But a book about what?" I asked.

"How long have you lived here in Mission?" he replied.

"Thirty-two years."

"Well, then."

It's an interesting community, Mission, where blue-collar values stand beside but do not always mix with a fierce dedication to the arts, where an economy still dependent on farming and forestry is increasingly hooked on the juggernaut of urban growth.

It's more interesting than Abbotsford, that's for sure, though it isn't always pretty. But then the last thing a photographer should want to do is make his subject pretty. Beautiful, yes. That's another matter. The thing about beauty, as the Romantic poets always said, is that the beautiful always contains elements of the dark and the unsavory. To respond to mere prettiness is to keep one's responses pretty much on the surface. To appreciate beauty is to respond to a wide and often discomfiting range of contrasts and possibilities.

Centennial Park in Mission is pretty. But do people actually *go* there? Mission as a whole, though, while it has attractive old hillside houses and stunning river views and sweeping mountain vistas and magnificent forest expanses right in its backyard, also has seedy back alleys and crapped-out shake mills and unkempt ravines where people dispose of their old tires, and a sometimes unpleasant (though hardly unique) history of dealing with non-Europeans.

The reason Stave Lake is such a beautiful place, though it

is far from being always pretty, has a lot to do with the fact that for half the year it's a shimmering expanse of pellucid and inviting blue water, but for the other half, the dark half, the interesting half of the year, the water level behind the dam is drawn down thirty or forty or fifty feet from summer recreational levels, and then all the reminders of dubious logging practices—the snags and spars and junked machinery that nobody back then took the trouble to take away—this brown mess is all out there in plain view. Until, that is, it all gets covered up again under the next spring's runoff. But just barely. Just enough that it will still tear the bottom out of your speedboat if you aren't paying close attention.

I have even run up on a stump in my kayak up there, and the last thing you want to do when you're paddling along with an expensive camera around your neck is to suddenly find yourself under water and upside down, hastily reviewing the procedure for a wet exit. This actually happened to me one day—not by tipping off a stump, and not at Stave Lake, but on the Fraser, where I believed I was clever enough and strong enough one lazy fall afternoon to muscle my way upstream past the end of what had once been a tree wedged firmly into the downstream end of a small sandbar.

Fifteen hundred dollars and a new camera later, I had learned my lesson.

But to take the pictures that you need to take, you need to take your camera with you wherever you go, certainly in your car and your boat, possibly even to bed. Most of the time when you take your camera out the door with you, nothing happens. But that one afternoon when you leave it at home because all you're doing is a quick run down to the grocery store anyway, for heaven's sake—that's when a troupe of Hare Krishnas stages an impromptu parade down Main Street, or the sky suddenly darkens and you get hail and weird blue clouds and impossibly orange trees, or an eighteen-wheeler loaded with ten thousand bright yellow rubber duckies spills its load across the entire width of the Mission Bridge.

In short, you have to have your eye as open as you can, and your equipment always at the ready. In some ways, it hardly matters what the subject matter is. Landscapes, streetscapes, water-scapes, skyscapes, people, buildings, trees, mailboxes, cardboard boxes, cats, graffiti, dead fish, steaming horses, shop windows, old tugboats—everything is grist for the mill, as long as the light is right. Reflected light, radiant light, natural light, artifical light, celestial light—the art of photography, as the etymology of the word makes clear, is really the art of drawing with light. People who take dull pictures in the flat, glaring light of the noonday sun are not necessarily dull people, nor even dull photographers; they just haven't yet learned to trust the evidence of their own eyes. One well-known photographer was asked why he took so many pictures all the time, and his reply was that he *liked to see what things looked like when they were photographed*. If you snap your shutter whilst aiming down at an otherwise unprepossessing pile of malodorous salmon early on a November morning when it actually feels as if this might look interesting when you see the finished product (for outdoor photography this usually means when the sun is at least semi-obscured or is not too far from the horizon), you stand a considerably better chance of getting a good picture than if you find yourself pointing your lens at a picturesque curve of the Great Wall of China on a cloudless day at one o'clock in the afternoon just because that's when the tour bus dropped you there.

In addition to subject matter and quality of light, there are also *formal* considerations, of course. Structure, composition, balance, all that. The best way to tell whether a photograph is *formally* pleasing, which means divesting it of as much content-related baggage as possible (does the bride really look as if she *likes* the groom; is aunt Vera actually *smiling*?) is to turn the picture upside down, or at least sideways. It's a bit like what the old eighteenth-century landscape painters did when they were sizing up a scene for its purely aesthetic possibilities: they turned around, bent over double, and looked at everything backwards and upside down through the framing device of their own two legs.

A word about the equipment used in the preparation of this book. Until recently, I shot everything with a 35 mm Canon EOS A2 single lens reflex camera on Fujichrome Velvia slide film (won-derfully fine grain, highly saturated colours). I used a 28 mm wide angle lens exclusively. To make digital files I scanned these slides (mostly on an Epson V750 scanner), then processed them in Adobe Photoshop (meaning, in this case, little more than getting the size right, removing dust spots and odd little smudges and worms, and tweaking brightness and contrast and sharpness a bit). Some of the most recent pictures were shot on a Canon 30D digital SLR with a 17-85 mm zoom. The book was laid out in Adobe InDesign.

Some of the book's images (and many more from other locales and on other topics) can also be viewed on my website, http://grahamdowden.ca. Anyone interested in purchasing additional copies of the book, or archival-quality inkjet prints in a variety of sizes and formats, should contact me, either via the website or at the Gyre & Gimble Publishers address listed on the copyright page.

An undertaking like this would have been utterly impossible without a huge amount of support. Over a hundred institutions and individuals had enough blind faith to contribute substantially to the project's costs. *Friends* (see the list at the back) are those who purchased at least one copy of the book well in advance of the publication date. *Patrons* (also listed at the back) contributed at a higher level, and *Angels* (see over) at a higher level yet. I must single out for its especially generous support my old employer and home away from home for 25 years, the University College of the Fraser Valley.

I am especially indebted to a few individuals without whom I would still be floundering around in the woulda shoulda coulda stages of all this: Jorge Rocha at Friesens; Kim Isaac and Rachele Oriente, who helped me with copyright; Bob McGregor and Geoff Fraser, who taught the software courses at UCFV and bailed me out on numerous occasions; Lynne Smith for her constant encouragement and marketing smarts; and above all my wife Judy Hill, whose technical wizardry and fearless criticism and inexhaustible fund of moral support still leave me at a loss for ... further ... words.

—Graham Dowden

ANGELS

Sophie Berner

Matt and Peggy Blackwood

(via Sharon Vallance)

(via Diane Griffiths)

the angel in the butcher shop window, december 2006

railway bridge, dean lauzé mural, october 2006

railway bridge with pigeons, september 2006

mission from the bridge, january 2006

westminster abbey grounds, january 1998

bell tower behind knoll, westminster abbey, january 1998

ukranian orthodox church, november 2006

mission city hall, december 2005

mission historical society, november 1977

mission sikh temple, september 2005

university college of the fraser valley, mission campus, january 2007

grotto of our lady of lourdes, november 1996

february 1997

january 2001

november 1998

17

sun on subdivision roofs, october 2006

heritage park place, november 1998

house under construction, september 2002

house with flaming sky, december 1998

everglades in flood, july 1997

everglades with alpenglow, december 2000

house on doyle street, november 2006

house on sylvester road, december 2006

house with smoke, december 2005

house in bright sun, march 2002

victorian house on stave lake road, december 2006

play house, ferndale, march 2002

my house in blizzard, november 1996

my back deck, november 2006

bungalow and mid-rise, march 2004

house with lattice and star, january 2000

house with suitcases, dewdney trunk road, april 1999

31

no clowns, september 2005

shopping carts, the junction, december 2006

advertising sign, london avenue, november 2006

main street hoarding, november 2006

ponder todays words, centennial park, november 2002

no. 10 hair design, june 2005

elvis of the bellevue, april 2005

junkie and dumpster, june 2005

japanese mural, railway avenue, january 2007

japanese mural, close up, january 2007

first nations mural, railway avenue, october 2003

first nations mural with dumpster, october 2003

unity pole, st mary's, january 2007

unity pole, close up, january 2007

angel in gift store window, december 2006

angel and receiver, november 2005

bird at rowena's, february 2004

red bird on fence, february 2000

hot dog, august 1997

horse and cat, january 2004

dead fish, november 2003

men fishing on stave river, november 2005

spawning salmon at weaver creek, november 1995

fish fence, e.s. richards school, october 2002

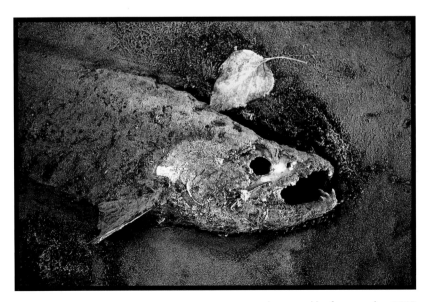

salmon and leaf, november 2003

53

memorial, matsqui prairie, january 2004

memorial, agassiz bridge, november 2006

fraser river, weird clouds, february 2000

fraser river, two suns, february 2000

fraser river, pilings in fog, september 2006

fraser river at whonnock, january 1998

fraser river from westminster abbey, january 1995

mission dock, high water, july 1997

matsqui cornfield, high water, june 2002

mission dock, low water, april 2001

matsqui cornfield, low water, february 2002

looking east from strawberry island, february 2001

sandbar below mission bridge, july 1998

fraser river with striking sky, march 2001

sumas mountain behind snag, september 2001

fraser river, boy pulling my kayak, august 1998

fraser river, approaching riffle, august 1998

fraser river, drifting home, september 1999

nicomen island, flooded woods, july 1999

nicomen slough in the rain, july 1997

nicomen slough at low water, november 2002

nicomen slough with deck chairs, march 2002

nicomen slough at sunset, march 2002

nicomen slough looking north up norrish valley, november 2000

mackerel sky over dewdney ridge, october 2000

near matsqui village, february 1999

stave lake from the air, february 2006

mt robie reid from the air, february 2006

stave lake, sayers point, november 2000

sayers point derrick, november 2000

cypress point, september 2002

stave lake, the narrows, september 2000

stave lake with water lilies, august 2002

stave lake, split snag, september 2001

stave lake, bare poles, september 2000

stave lake, birdlike snag, august 2000

stave lake, south end, september 1999

stave lake from the dam, november 2006

m. v. shirley, stave falls, november 2006

sea imp XIX, september 2006

spiderwebs on wreckage, september 2006

hatzic prairie community hall, december 2006

mission rod and gun club, november 2006

gate, stave lake road, december 2005

blue fairlane, cherry avenue, november 2004

icebound truck, matsqui village, january 2004

old faithful III, january 2003

car seat in woods, december 2002

wuz up, october 2002

rocket man, mission raceway, october 2006

dark energy, mission raceway, october 2006

rapid fire, mission raceway, october 2006

smokin' olds, mission raceway, october 2006

pit crew, mission raceway, october 2006

santa, clayburn village, january 2000

maroon car, clayburn village, november 2005

matsqui prairie greenhouse at dawn, november 2005

matsqui prairie greenhouse interior, november 1998

farm house, matsqui prairie, january 2002

floodlights and dewdney ridge, december 1996

cottonwood plantation, strawberry island, december 1999

harrison hot springs, october 2000

statue emporium, agassiz, january 2007

virgin and barbed wire, agassiz, january 2007

abbotsford-mission highway, december 2006

snowscape, ferndale avenue, january 2003

ferndale avenue at draper street, january 2003

frozen ditch, hatzic prairie, march 2002

greenhouses, hatzic prairie, march 2002

red barn, sylvester road, january 2005

red barn, stave lake road, december 2003

barn, farms road, october 2006

farmer len, mount lehman, november 2003

number 45, nicomen island, september 1997

morning fireball, mount lehman, september 2001

sign, harris road, matsqui, july 2004

clubhouse, eighteen pastures golf course, november 2005

golfer in mist, eighteen pastures, november 2005

ninth hole, eighteen pastures, january 2002

fourth green, eighteen pastures, december 2001

cart in pond, eighteen pastures, december 2004

mailbox as tractor, january 2004

mailbox as skier, january 2004

bandaged mailbox, december 2003

mailbox with spots, january 2004

mailbox as parrot, january 2004

mailboxes with pig, fish, and ducks, january 2004

mailbox with tire track, january 2004

fortune teller, renaissance fayre, july 2002

conversation, renaissance fayre, july 2002

infant perusing program, mission folk music festival, july 1997

daytime stage, mission folk music festival, july 1999

gaggle of kids, mission folk music festival, july 1996

boy with gizmo, mission folk music festival, july 1997

girls dancing, frankie lee singing, mission folk music festival, july 2000

woman dancing, mission folk music festival, july 1996

man dancing, mission folk music festival, july 2002

the girl in the blue skirt, mission folk music festival, july 2002

PATRONS

Rosemary Caskey

Lori Charvat & Sheila Woody

Doyle & Margaret Clifton

Graham T. Cocksedge

Ted & Rosemary Cragg

Marg Esch

John Foy

Judy Hill

Kim Isaac

Donna & John Johannessen

Wayne Lindberg

Virginia O'Brien

Alex Robbins

Lynne Smith

Mary Tilberg

Betty-Joan & Lionel Traverse

UCFV Bookstore

FRIENDS OF THE PROJECT

Michelle Adams

Pam Alexis

Kim Allen

Roy & Olive Anderson (née Horvath)

Mark Angelo

Graham & Debra Archer

Barb & Dick Bate

Valerie Billesberger

Carlo Billinger

Bill & Jane Bisson

Tom Bjerke & Bonnie Lowinske

Cathy Bonnett

Naomi Born

Arlene Boudreau

Fr. Abbot John Braganza

Ian Brooks

Kevin Busswood

Liz & Duncan Campbell

Susan (née Dowden) & Duncan Campbell

Sherry Cannon

Myra Christopherson

Keith & Verna Clarke

Trish & Graham Cocksedge

Wendy Cocksedge

Dick & Phyllis Cooke

Virginia Cooke & John Potts

Cheryl Dahl

Grace Dahl

Karin & Ron Dart

Jane & John Dean

Melinda Dempster

District of Mission

Liz Ellis

Jim & Diana Foy

Fraser Basin Council

Fraser River Wines

Bonnie Gabel

Laura, Dean, Liam, & Olivia Gottfried

Deb & Keith Greenfield

Véronique Guillet

Robert Gunn

Clint & Laura Hames

Heather & August Hansson

Madeleine Hardin

Reimar Hauschildt & Susan Daly

John Harris

Pat Harris

Vicki Hick

Marcia Horricks & John Grieve

Rob Horricks & Rachele Oriente

Valerie Hundert

Sheila Jeck & David Moon

Barry & Carol Johnston

Maniam & Co Kuppusami

Catherine McDonald

Marilyn McDonald

Darren McFadden (in memory of Buster)

Adri & Pierre Marais

Cathie & Jim Marcellus

Rick Mawson

Joanne Mills

Mission Community Archives

Mission Teachers' Union

Ann & Gordon Mohs

Diana Muntigl & Ron Coreau

Audrey Neufeld

Christine Newsome

Sue Nicholson

Grant & Susan Perry

Rhian Piprell

June Reedman (in memory of Lew Vaughan)

Colin Ridgewell

Mike & Mary Robbins

Juliette Robertson

Marion Robinson

Robert Ross & Mary Ediger

Gordon Ruley

Karen Saenger

Andreas Schroeder & Sharon Brown

George & Bonnie Sigaty

Heather Stewart

Mia Thomas

Diana Lynn Thompson

Guy & Susan Thorne

Darlene Till

Christina Toth

Susan Underwood

UCFV Library Heritage Collection

Duane Wall

Karolle Wall

Cathy Waller

Bob Warick

Des & Ivy Winterbottom

Leslie Wood

Dave Wyatt (for Mike Dempster)